BRANCH LINES AROUND CLEOBURY MORTIMER

Vic Mitchell and Keith Smith

MP Middleton Press

Published October 2007

ISBN 978 1 906008 18 5

© Middleton Press, 2007

Design Deborah Esher
Typesetting Barbara Mitchell

Published by
 Middleton Press
 Easebourne Lane
 Midhurst
 West Sussex
 GU29 9AZ
Tel: 01730 813169
Fax: 01730 812601
Email: info@middletonpress.co.uk
www.middletonpress.co.uk

Printed & bound by Biddles Ltd, Kings Lynn

CONTENTS

INDEX

ACKNOWLEDGEMENTS

We are very grateful for the assistance received from many of those mentioned in the credits also to W.R.Burton, A.R.Carder, L.Crosier, G.Croughton, M.Dart, S.C.Jenkins, D.K.Jones, N.Langridge, B.Lewis, Mr D. and Dr S.Salter, G.T.V.Stacey, P.Q.Treloar, D.C.Williams, E.Wilmshurst and in particular, our always supportive wives, Barbara Mitchell and Janet Smith.

I. Railway Clearing House map showing the branch names when opened.

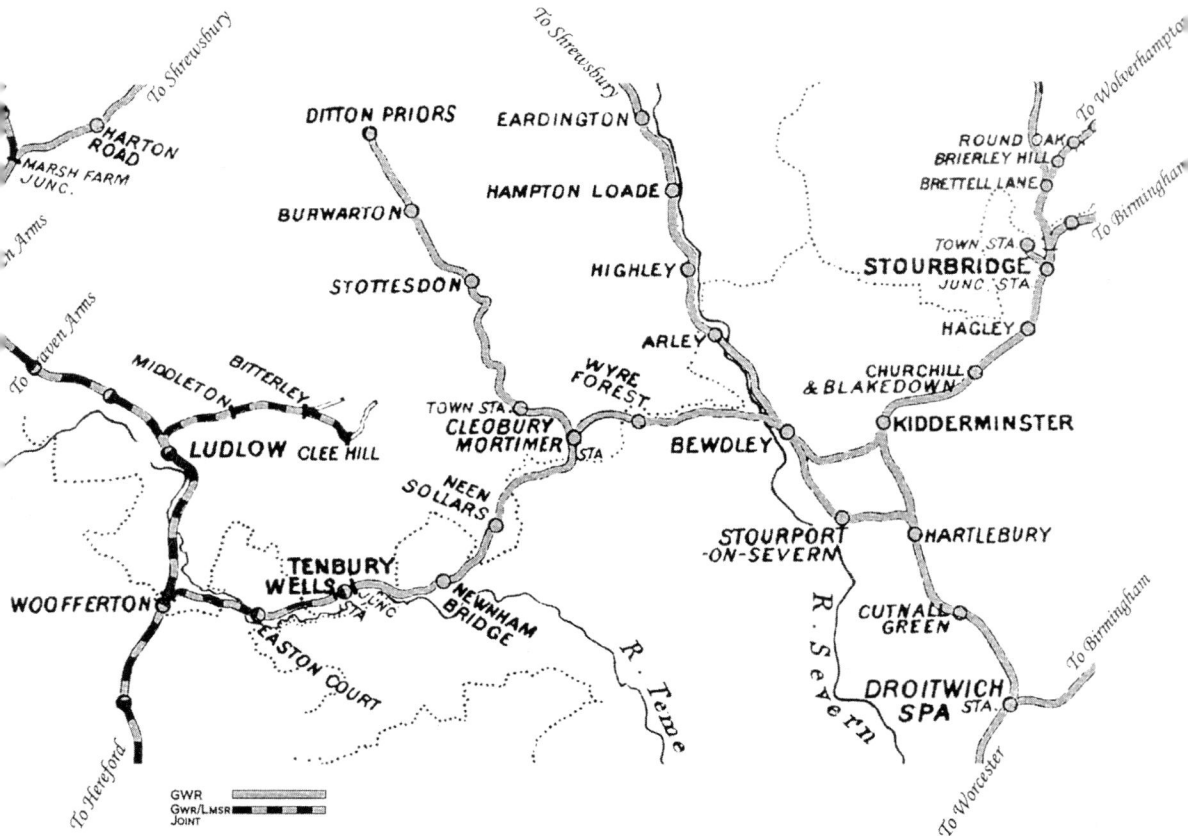

GEOGRAPHICAL SETTING

The route from Woofferton followed the east flowing River Teme as far as Newnham Bridge and then the south flowing River Rea to Cleobury Mortimer. Lower Old Red Sandstone is the underlying feature of this section and also much of the line to Ditton Priors. This was in close proximity to the River Rea and a tributary of it, the Moor Brook. Limestone and Basalt in the Clee Hills was of economic importance and provided rail traffic. There was also some coal in the area.

The route between Cleobury Mortimer and Bewdley descended through the Wyre Forest to run close to the Dowles Brook, which flows into the River Severn near the line's bridge over it.

The east-west route crossed in and out of Worcestershire and Shropshire, whereas the branch north was entirely in the latter county.

The maps are to the scale of 25ins to 1 mile, with north at the top, unless otherwise indicated. Sadly, the short life of the Ditton Priors branch meant that it did not appear on any OS editions at this scale.

Down trains were from Woofferton to Bewdley from 1878 to 1948, but it was reversed thereafter.

II. The 1946 edition at 4 miles to 1ins has Ditton Priors at the top, but no branch stations are shown. The dark patches to the left of the line are the two Clee Hills.

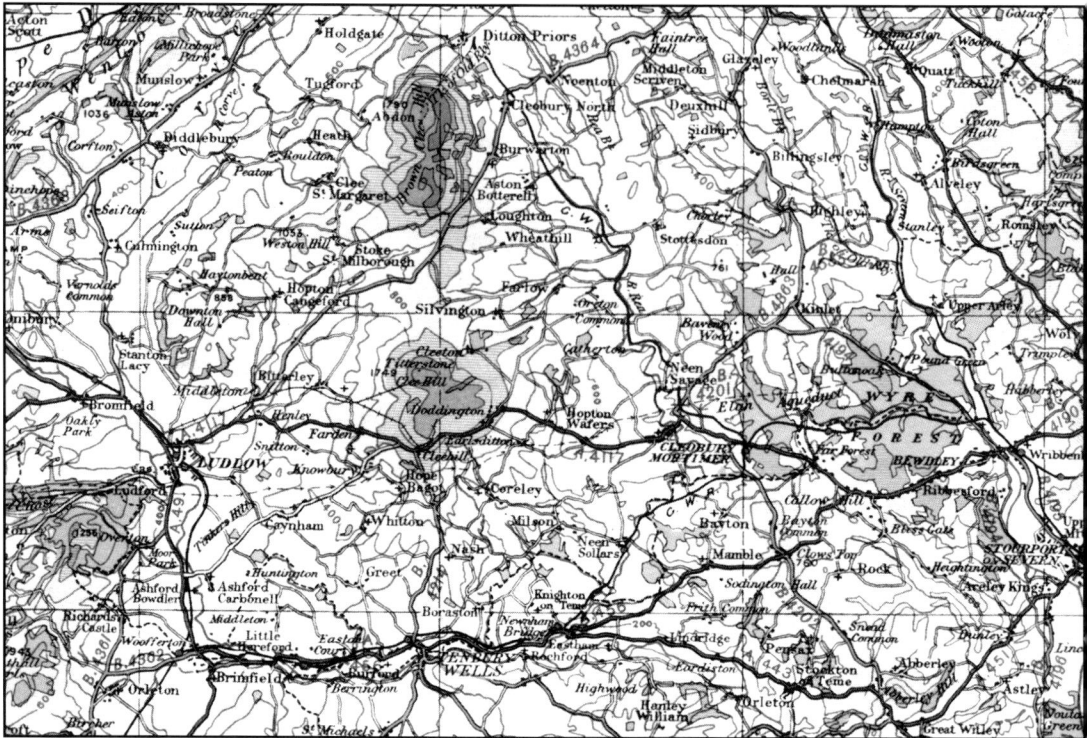

III. Gradient profile for Bewdley-Tenbury.

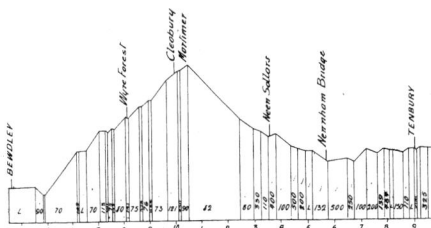

IV. Gradient profile for the Ditton Priors branch.

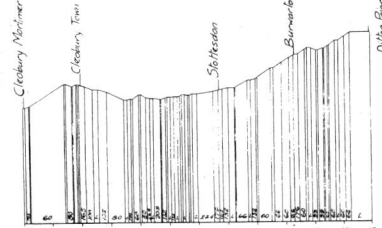

HISTORICAL BACKGROUND

The first railway in the area was the Shrewsbury & Hereford, opening in 1853 south of Ludlow. The Great Western Railway and the London & North Western Railway became joint owners in 1870 and the former acquired the 1862 Severn Valley Railway in 1872. This branched from the main line at Hartlebury and it was to be 1878 before the Bewdley-Kidderminster link was completed.

The Act for the Tenbury Railway was passed on 21st July 1859 and it opened from Woofferton to Tenbury on 1st August 1861. It became joint GWR/LNWR property in 1869 having been leased since 1862 and worked by the LNWR.

The Tenbury & Bewdley Railway opened on 13th August 1864 and that line was acquired by the GWR in 1870. Its Act had been passed on 3rd July 1860.

A Light Railway Order was obtained by local businessmen for the Cleobury Mortimer & Ditton Priors Light Railway on 23rd March 1901, but the line did not come into use until 21st November 1908, for passengers (1st July for goods).

The Clee Hill Granite Company was connected to Dettonford by an aerial ropeway from its quarry in Titterstone Clee Hill, but this was worked out by 1928. The Abdon Clee Quarry Company had a rope-worked incline to Ditton Priors station and produced dhustone, mainly for roadmaking, but this traffic ceased in 1936.

The branch had become part of the GWR on 25th May 1922 and the passenger service was withdrawn on 26th September 1938. A degree of prosperity returned to the line when the Royal Navy Armaments Depot was opened in mid-June 1941. Local goods traffic had been suspended after the onset of war, on 11th September 1939, and was never restored. There were no other changes until nationalisation in 1948, when the GWR became the Western Region of British Railways. The lines in the area were transferred to the London Midland Region on 1st January 1963.

All services between Woofferton and Tenbury Wells were withdrawn on 31st July 1961. Passenger trains were withdrawn between Tenbury Wells and Bewdley on 1st August 1962, but freight continued until 6th January 1964, west of Cleobury Mortimer. The Ditton Priors branch was transferred to the Admiralty on 1st May 1957 and the line was closed totally on 16th April 1965, together with the route east of Cleobury Mortimer.

The Severn Valley Railway Society was formed on 6th July 1965 to reopen the line between Hampton Loade and Bridgnorth. This was achieved on 23rd May 1970, coal traffic south of Alveley having ceased in 1969. The SVR became a company in 1967 and pursued the purchase of the route south to Foley Park.

The train service was extended from Hampton Loade to Highley on 12th April 1974 and on to Bewdley on 18th May of that year. Extension to Kidderminster took place on 30th July 1984.

The BR service between Hartlebury and Kidderminster via Stourport had been withdrawn on 5th January 1970.

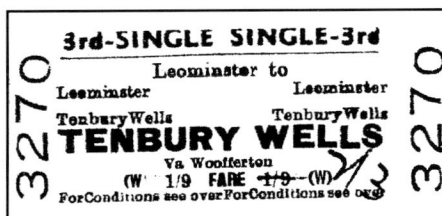

3270 — 3rd-SINGLE SINGLE-3rd
Leominster to
Leominster   Leominster
Tenbury Wells   Tenbury Wells
TENBURY WELLS — 3270
Va Woofferton
(W 1/9 FARE 1/9 (W)
For Conditions see over For Conditions see over

PASSENGER SERVICES

Woofferton to Bewdley

We have no evidence of Sunday trains running.

The initial timetable showed five trains per day on the five mile branch to Tenbury, this increasing to six in 1863. The 1869 timetable had just three trains serving all stations on the extended route. By 1889, this figure was four.

Twenty years later, there were six trips over the entire route, with four more west of Tenbury. The same still applied in 1950, although one short working had been lost.

The 1960 timetable showed only two through services, plus four west of Tenbury Wells and three east thereof. The final "experimental" timetable offered just one train between Tenbury Wells and Kidderminster, Mondays to Fridays only.

Ditton Priors Branch

For most of the life of the line, only two return trips were operated, weekdays only. Some trains did not run south of Cleobury Town and some would wait there for an hour or so. During World War I and until at least 1922, services were operated on Mondays, Wednesdays and Fridays only.

June 1869

WOOFFERTON, TENBURY, and BEWDLEY.

March 1909

KIDDERMINSTER, BEWDLEY, TENBURY, and WOOFFERTON.—Great Western.

March 1909

CLEOBURY MORTIMER, STOTTESDON, and DITTON PRIORS.—
Cleobury Mortimer and Ditton Priors Light.

June 1922

KIDDERMINSTER, BEWDLEY, TENBURY WELLS, and WOOFFERTON.—Great Western.

Miles	Up.	Week Days only.							
		mrn	mrn	mrn	aft	aft	aft	aft	aft
—	Kidderminster ....dep.	....	8 50	1020	1 55	....	4 40	5 55	....
3¼	Bewdley 90, 91 .... arr.	....	8 58	1028	2 3	....	4 48	6 3	....
	dep.	....	9 0	1033	2 10	....	4 51	6 6	....
8	Wyre Forest	....	9 11	1046	2 21	....	5 2	b	....
10	Cleobury Mortimer 118 ..	....	9 20	1053	2 29	....	5 10	6 25	....
13¼	Neen Sollars	....	9 28	11 0	2 37	....	5 18	6 32	....
15¾	Newnham Bridge	....	9 33	11 5	2 45	....	5 24	6 37	....
19	Tenbury Wells..... arr.	....	9 39	1111	2 52	....	5 30	6 49	....
	dep.	7 30	9 42	1114	3 0	4 35	5 35	6 53	8 5
21½	Easton Court ‖	7 36	9 48	1120	3 6	4 41	5 41	6 59	8 11
24¼	Woofferton 450, 452.arr.	7 42	9 54	1126	3 12	4 47	5 47	7 5	8 17

Miles	Down.	Week Days only.								
		mrn	mrn	mrn	mrn	aft	aft	aft	aft	aft
—	Woofferton ....dep.	7 8	8 15	1015	1150	3 55	4 15	5 10	6 15	7 40
2¾	Easton Court ‖	7 15	8 22	1022	1157	4 1	4 21	5 16	6 21	7 47
5¼	Tenbury Wells..... arr.	7 20	8 27	1027	12 2	4 7	4 26	5 21	6 27	7 52
	dep.	....	8 42	1030	1213	4 10	....	....	6 50	....
8½	Newnham Bridge	....	8 50	1038	1221	4 19	....	....	6 58	....
10¾	Neen Sollars	....	9 3	1044	1227	4 26	....	....	7 4	....
14¼	Cleobury Mortimer 118 ...	....	9 17	1058	1238	4 37	....	....	7 15	....
16¼	Wyre Forest	....	9 25	11 3	1243	4 42	....	....	b	....
20¾	Bewdley 90, 91..... arr.	....	9 34	1112	1252	4 50	....	....	7 28	....
	dep.	....	9 37	1123	1 0	4 57	....	....	7 31	....
24¼	Kidderminster 96 ....arr.	....	9 45	1131	1 8	5 6	....	....	7 41	....

NOTES.

b Stops at Wyre Forest to set down only.

‖ Station for Little Hereford (½ mile).

March 1938

CLEOBURY MORTIMER and DITTON PRIORS HALT.

Miles	Down.	Week Days only.						
		mrn		Wednesdays only. aft		aft	
	Cleobury Mortimer.dep.	9 30	..	2 24	..	5 20	..
2	Cleobury Town Halt arr.	9 40	..	2 34	..	5 28	..
	dep.	9 48	..	2 39	..	5 29	..
4¼	Detton Ford Siding	9A58	..	2A48	..	5A 6	..
5¼	Prescott Siding	10A 5	..	2A53	..	5A40	..
6¼	Stottesdon Halt	10 11	..	3 1	..	5 45	..
8½	Aston Botterell Siding...	10A20	..	3A13	..	5A56	..
9	Burwarton Halt	10 29	..	3 19	..	5 57	..
10¼	Cleobury North Crossing..	10A40	..	3A27	..	6A 4	..
12	Ditton Priors Halt..arr.	10 48	..	3 36	..	6 11	..

Miles	Up.	Week Days only.						
		mrn		Wednesdays only. aft		aft	
	Ditton Priors Halt ....dep.	11 10	..	3 50	..	6 23	..
1¾	Cleobury North Crossing ...	11A16	..	3A53	..	6A25	..
2¾	Burwarton Halt	11 23	..	4 3		6 32	..
3½	Aston Botterell Siding	11A27	..	..	..	..	..
5¼	Stottesdon Halt	11 35	..	4 13	..	6 43	..
6¼	Prescott Siding	11A40	..	..	..	..	..
7¾	Detton Ford Siding	11A48	..	4A24	..	6A52	..
10	Cleobury Town Halt.. arr.	12 5	..	4 34	..	7 2	..
	dep.	12 10	..	4 41	..	7 4	..
12	Cleobury Mortimer 136 ar.	12 20	..	4 58	..	7 14	..

A Stop when required.

June 1950

WOOFFERTON, TENBURY WELLS, BEWDLEY, and KIDDERMINSTER

Miles	Week Days only														
		a.m 3	a.m X	a.m 3	a.m	a.m X	p.m X	p.m 3	p.m	p.m S					
	Woofferton .... dep	7 40	8 9	8 30	10 5	1155	3 47	4 30	7 50	9 45	..	..	..	..	..
2¾	Easton Court B........	7 46	8 15	8 36	1011	12 0	3 53	4 36	7 56	9 51	..	..	..	..	..
5¼	Tenbury Wells... arr	7 50	8 19	8 40	1015	12 5	3 57	4 40	8 0	9 55	..	..	..	..	..
	dep	..	8 20	..	1020	1213	4 0	..	8 2	10 0	..	..	..	..	..
8½	Newnham Bridge	..	8 28	..	1028	1222	4 8	..	8 10	10 7	..	..	..	..	..
10¾	Neen Sollars...........	..	8 34	..	1034	1228	4 14	..	8 16	1013	..	..	..	..	..
14¼	Cleobury Mortimer.....	..	8 44	..	1048	1238	4 23	..	8 26	1024	..	..	..	..	..
16¼	Wyre Forest...........	..	8 49	..	1053	1244	4 28	..	8 31	..	..	..	..	..	..
20¾	Bewdley.......... arr	..	8 57	..	11 1	1253	4 36	..	8 39	1038	..	..	..	..	..
	dep	..	9 0	..	11 3	1 2	4 48	..	8 41	1043	..	..	..	..	..
22¾	Foley Park Halt........	..	9 5	..	11 8	1 7	4 53	..	8 46	..	..	..	..	..	..
24¼	Kidderminster...... arr	..	9 10	..	1112	1 11	4 57	..	8 50	1055	..	..	..	..	..

B Station for Little Hereford (½ mile). S Saturdays only. X Third class only, limited accommodation. 3 Third class only.

June 1962

KIDDERMINSTER, BEWDLEY and TENBURY WELLS
MONDAYS TO FRIDAYS ONLY Second class only

Miles		pm						
—	**Kidderminster** .. dep	**4 10**	..	..	..	..	..	..
1½	Foley Park Halt..........	4 14	..	..	..	..	..	..
3½	**Bewdley** .. .. arr	4 19	..	..	..	..	..	..
	dep	4 20	..	..	..	..	..	..
8	Wyre Forest	4 30	..	..	..	..	..	..
10	Cleobury Mortimer	4 36	..	..	..	..	..	..
13½	Neen Sollars	4 42	..	..	..	..	..	..
15¾	Newnham Bridge	4 47	..	..	..	..	..	..
19	**Tenbury Wells** .. arr	**4 53**	..	..	..	..	..	..

	am								
Tenbury Wells .. dep	**7 55**	..	..	..	..	..	..	..	..
Newnham Bridge	8 3	..	..	..	..	..	..	..	..
Neen Sollars	8 8	..	..	..	..	..	..	..	..
Cleobury Mortimer	8 21	..	..	..	..	..	..	..	..
Wyre Forest..	8 26	..	..	..	..	..	..	..	..
Bewdley .. .. arr	8 34	..	..	..	..	..	..	..	..
dep	8 35	..	..	..	..	..	..	..	..
Foley Park Halt..........	8 40	..	..	..	..	..	..	..	..
Kidderminster .. arr	**8 44**	..	..	..	..	..	..	..	..

July 1918

CLEOBURY MORTIMER and DITTON PRIORS.—Cleobury Mortimer and Ditton Priors Light.
Gen. Man., E. J. Morris, Cleobury Mortimer.

Miles	Down.	Week Days only.			
		Mons. & Weds. mrn	Weds., Fris., & Sats. aft		
	Cleobury Mortimer..dep.	9 19	2 25	....	....
2	Cleobury Town ¶... arr.	9 32	2 38	....	....
	dep.	9 35	2 45	....	....
6¾	Stottesdon ¶............	10 0	3 10	....	....
9½	Burwarton ¶............	1015	3 25	....	....
12	Ditton Priors ....arr.	1033	3 45	....	....

Miles	Up.	Week Days only.			
		Mons. & Weds. mrn	Weds., Fris., & Sats. aft		
	Ditton Priors ¶........dep.	11 5	4 10	....	....
2½	Burwarton ¶............	1120	4 24	....	....
5¼	Stottesdon ¶............	1134	4 38	....	....
10	Cleobury Town....... arr.	12 5	5 15	....	....
	dep.	12 6	....	....	....
12	Cleobury Mortimer 107 arr	1222	....	....	....

¶ "Halts," at Chilton, Detton Ford, and Prescott Sidings, between Cleobury Town and Stottesdon; Aston Botterell Siding, between Stottesdon and Burwarton; and Cleobury North Crossing, between Burwarton and Ditton Priors.

1. Woofferton to Bewdley

WOOFFERTON

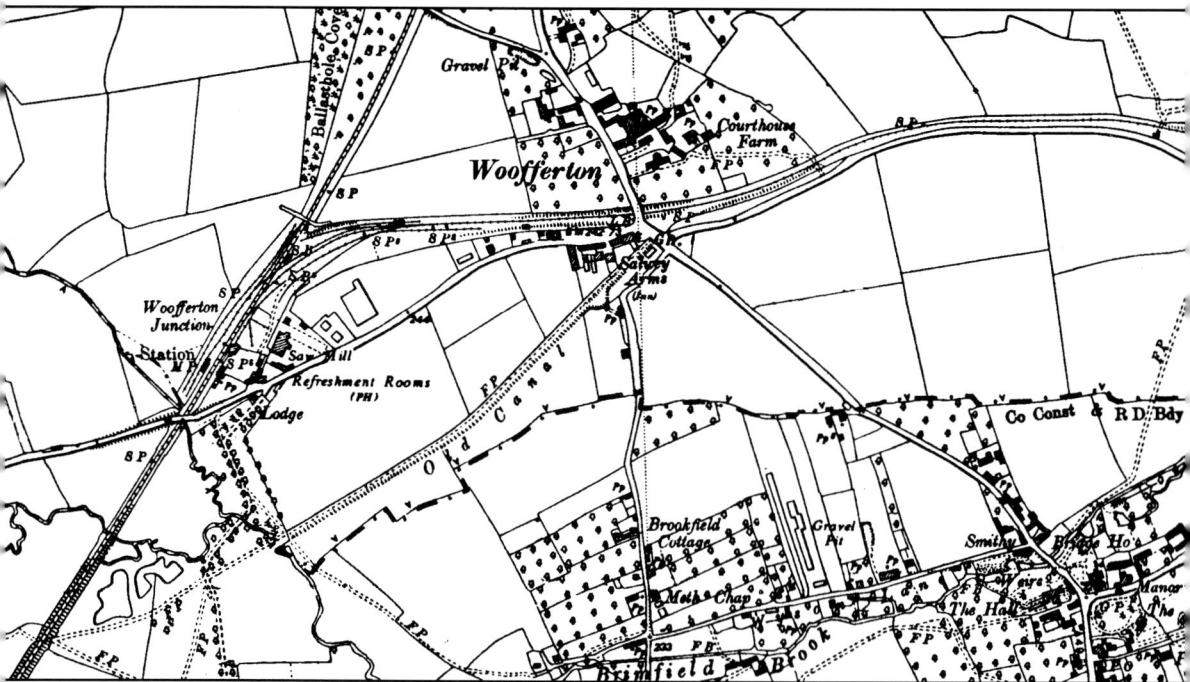

V.   The 1952 map at 6 ins to 1 mile has the main line from Shrewsbury and Ludlow at the top and the single line to Tenbury Wells on the right. It is evident that part of the branch was built on the route of a canal, namely the Kington, Leominster & Stourport Canal. The "Refreshment Rooms" were run by the local landlord, not the railway.

1.   Two northward panoramas give an introductory overview of the station. This one is from the road bridge in about 1923. It carried the B4302, so numbered in 1919. (Stations UK)

2.   This view is from the footbridge in 1949 and shows more clearly the bay platform for branch trains and the connection over two diamond crossings in the main lines. This was removed on 17th November 1957, as were the two sidings on the left. (J.Moss/R.S.Carpenter coll.)

3.   The bay was known as "Back Platform" and was added in 1889, as were the adjacent sidings. A small crowd joins the branch train on 10th September 1949. (H.C.Casserley)

VI.   The 1903 survey has the ballast pit sidings top left and the engine shed on the right. This closed in November 1896, but remained standing until about 1960, as part of it supported the water tank.

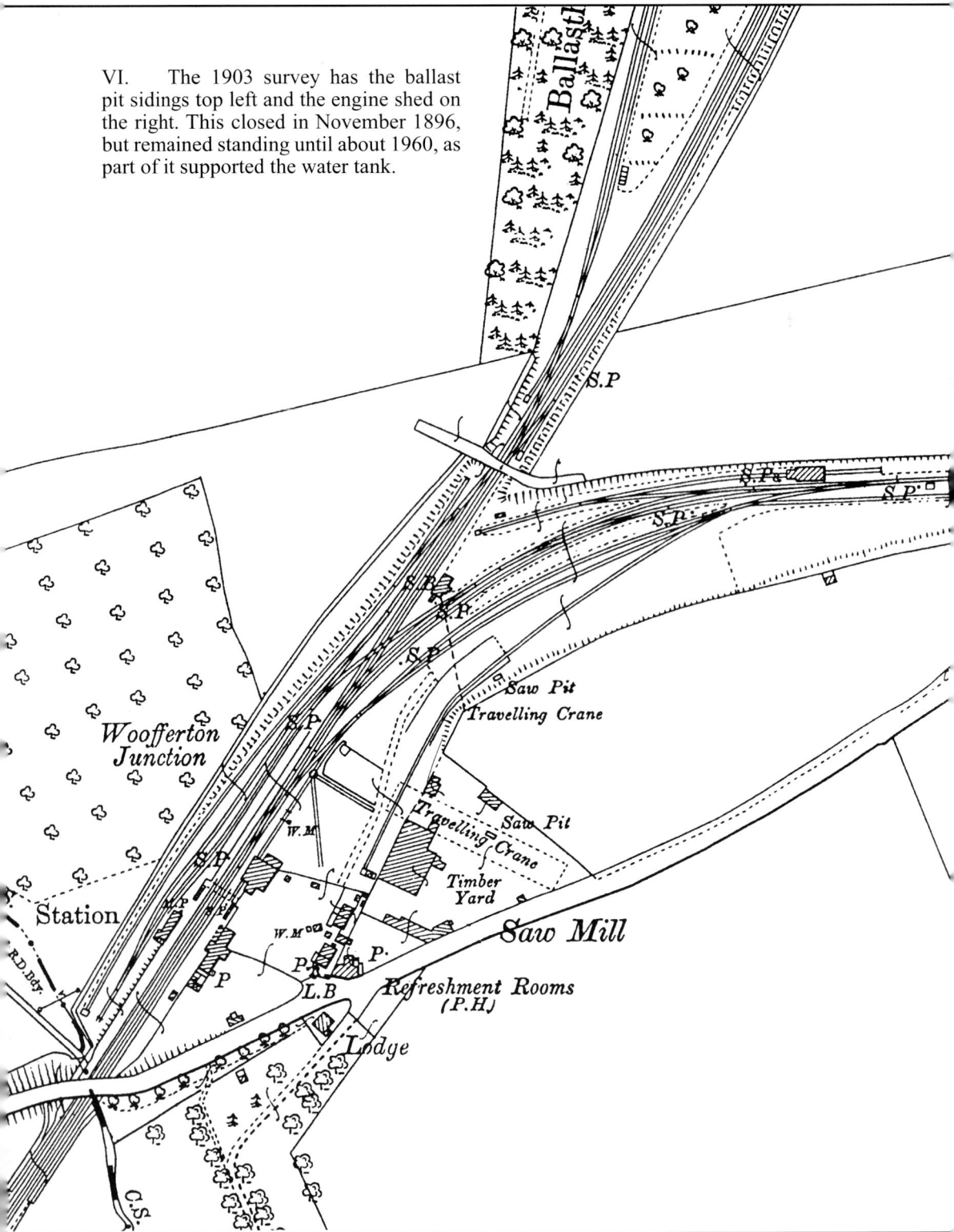

Ballast

S.P

S.P.

S.P.

S.P

S.P.

S.P.

S.P

Saw Pit

Travelling Crane

Woofferton
Junction

W.M

Travelling Crane

Saw Pit

Timber
Yard

Station

W.M

Saw Mill

P.

P

P.

L.B

Refreshment Rooms
(P.H.)

R.D.Bdy.

Lodge

C.S.

4.   A view north from the bay on 27th July 1957 features the run-round loop adjacent to the platform road. Next to that is the up refuge siding, in which a coal train stands. (R.M.Casserley)

5.   A mailbag approaches the up platform at the end of which a sign states NO ROAD. The railcar is leaving the branch on 22nd March 1958. (G.Adams/M.J.Stretton coll.)

6. No. 6862 *Derwent Grange* is working hard on the approach to a length of 1 in 100 up gradient sometime in 1961. Alongside it is a shunt signal, with route indicator. (J.Moss/ R.S.Carpenter coll.)

7. The route indicator links were evident on the left as 0-4-2T no. 1445 stands with the branch train on 24th June 1961. The word JUNCTION appeared on the nameboards, but not on timetables and tickets. (G.Adams/M.J.Stretton coll.)

8.   The same train is waiting on the curve to form the 5.25pm to Tenbury Wells on 1st April 1961. The former bay was used as a refuge siding at that time. The bridge simply joined two fields. (J.Langford)

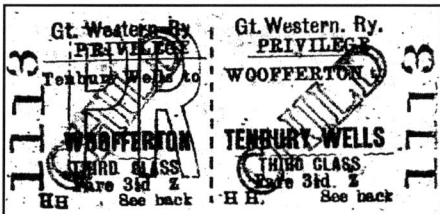

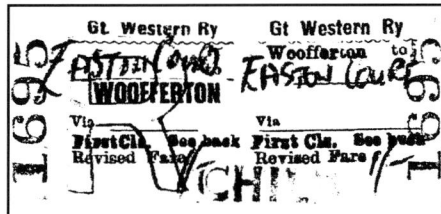

9.   There were signs for GENTLEMEN on both platforms, plus provision for cloaks. The perforated shunt signal is clear as parcel traffic is handled in 1961. Oil lamps lasted to the end. (J.Peden/Stations UK)

Other views of this station can be found in our *Ludlow to Hereford* **album in pictures 8 to 18.**

10.   The down building is seen shortly after passenger service was withdrawn on 31st July 1961. Freight facilities continued here until 7th October 1963. (Lens of Sutton coll.)

11.   Sprinter no. 156465 was working the 11.02 service from Swansea to Manchester on 10th May 1989. The accommodation bridge for the farm had gone, but the 39-lever signal box, the up loop and the goods shed could still be seen. (P.G.Barnes)

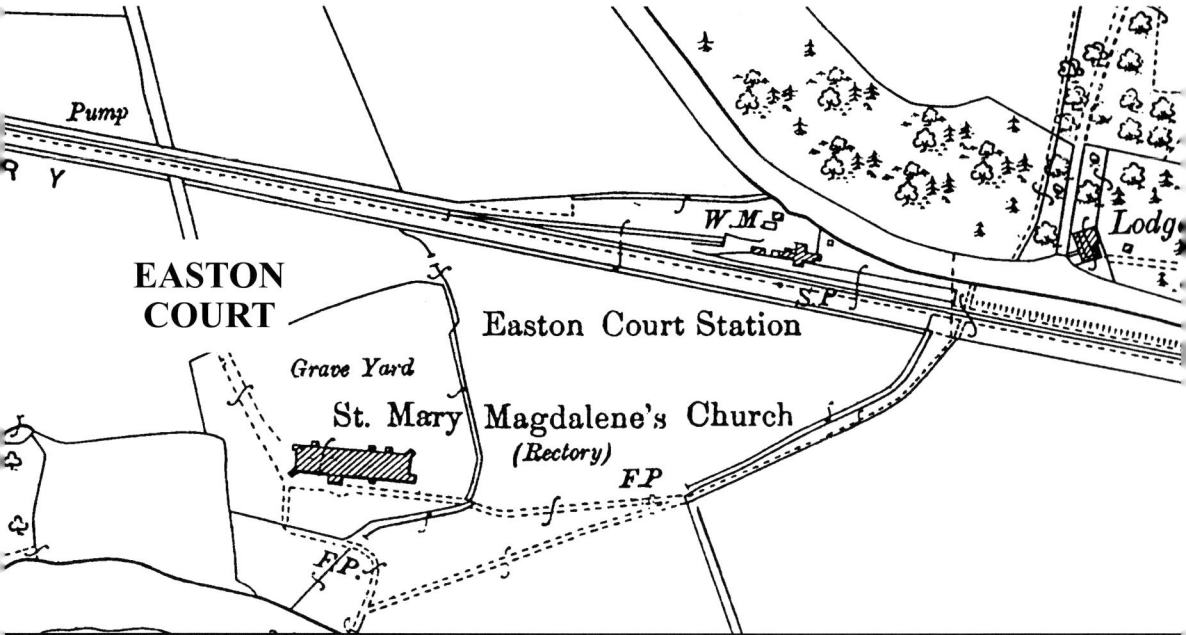

Pump

EASTON COURT

Easton Court Station

Grave Yard

St. Mary Magdalene's Church

(Rectory)

W.M.^S

S.P.

Lodg

FP

FP

FP

VII.   The station opened with the line, but closed in October 1862 as it was generating less than 15 shillings per week. However, its use by the local landowner continued and a coal merchant arrived. It reopened to the public in April 1865, eight months after the line to Bewdley was completed. The gate to Easton Court is on the right on this 1903 map.

12.   The flags were out to celebrate the end of the Boer War in June 1902. The name "Little Hereford" was added to the nameboard, but not the timetables, in November 1889. (A.Dudman coll.)

13.   The north elevation was recorded in the mid-1920s. Soon, the staffing level was halved, to one. Another modest improvement in 1889 had been the provision of a weighing machine in the goods yard, W.M. on the map. (A.Dudman coll.)

14.   Facilities were limited and the plan for a ladies room in 1912 was rejected as too expensive, as was a second siding for timber traffic. The 4.30pm Woofferton to Tenbury Wells is waiting on 18th August 1956. This train started at Craven Arms at 4.5 and called at Ludlow at 4.20 for school pupils. (Stephenson Locomotive Society)

15. Staff shortage in World War II brought 73 year-old John Morgan out of retirement to work here until he was 78. With low evening sun, a green-painted railcar waits for the photographer to board again. (Stations UK)

16. Staffing ceased in September 1954, but the house continued to be occupied by railway employees. The loading gauge was another 1889 addition. This westward view is from 6th July 1961, three weeks before total closure. (R.G.Nelson/T.Walsh)

TENBURY WELLS

VIII.   The boundary between the joint line and the GWR was near the right border of this 1903 map and the boundary between the counties is shown with dots and dashes. A 4-ton crane was provided later. The 15-lever West signal box is lower left.

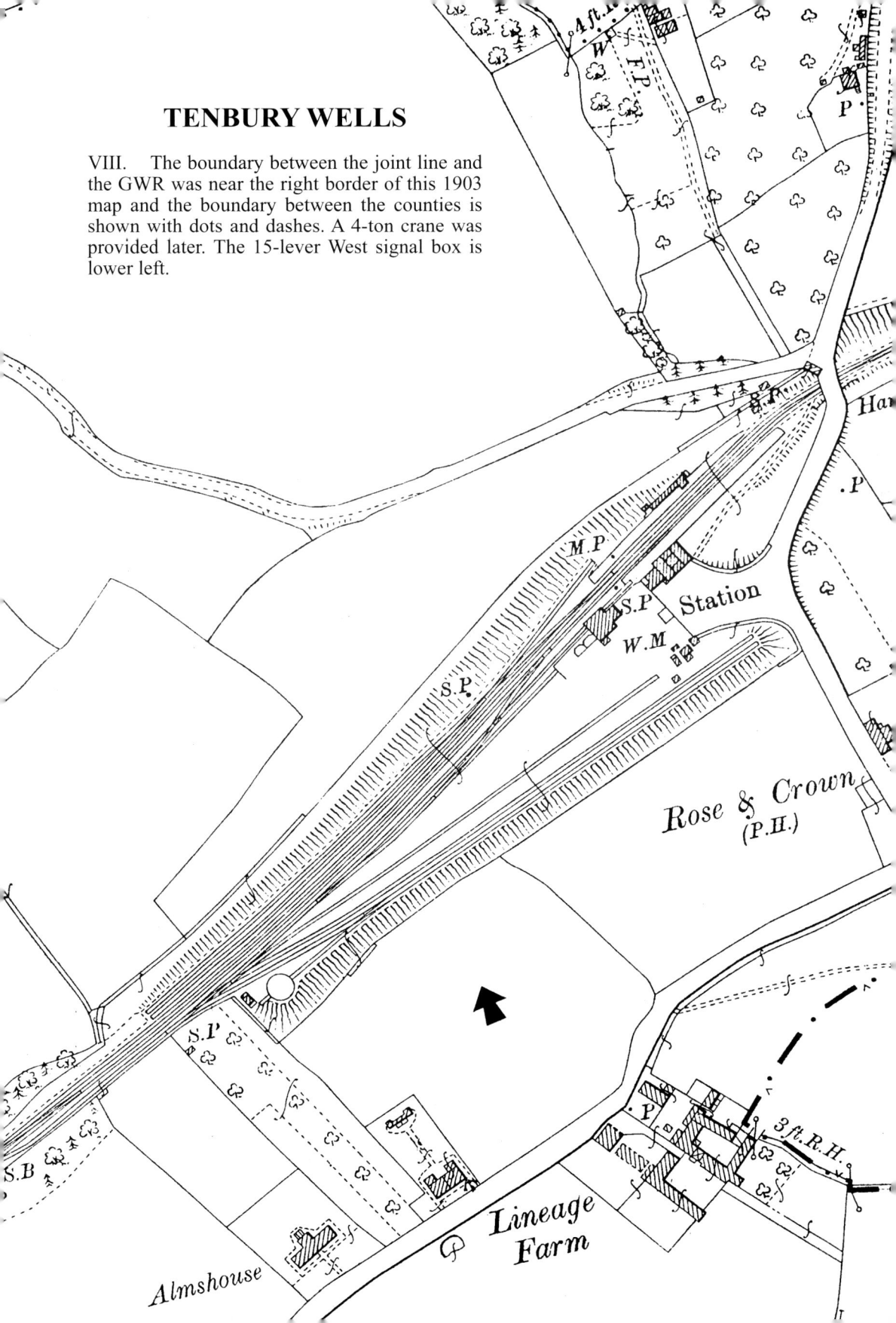

17.   The cattle pens in the foreground were 1913 additions; there were 17 men here at that time. The first Sunday excursion coincided with an earthquake in May 1925. It removed chimney pots and derailed wagons. A class 517 0-4-2T is arriving in the Edwardian era. (Lens of Sutton coll.)

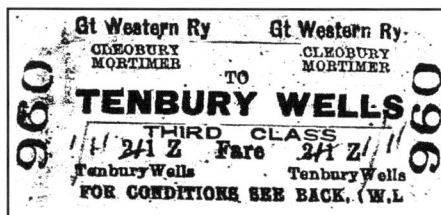

18.   The station was served by a steam railmotor (left) running between Hereford and Stourbridge for several years from 1906. Second class travel was possible westwards until 1st July 1910 and eastwards until 1st October of that year, this reflecting the different ownerships of the route. (Lens of Sutton coll.)

19.   The Tenbury Wells Aerated Water Company despatched its fruit drinks in quantity from 1895. Fresh fruit and dead rabbits were frequently loaded onto passenger trains here. The LNWR built West or "B" Box and it was in the distance until its closure on 12th October 1928. There is evidence of the 1911 platform lengthening. (J.Moss/R.S.Carpenter)

20.   Holly and mistletoe made up other seasonal traffic here, as did poultry, alive and dead. Railcar no. 27 is seen on 26th August 1949. From 1950, the Worcester car ran empty to Ludlow via Shelwick Junction and then worked all Tenbury trips, except one autotrain working from Leominster and two trips operated from Kidderminster. (B.W.L.Brooksbank)

GW&LM&S.RlysJt   GW&LM&S.RlysJt
Tenbury Wells   Tenbury Wells
                TO
    Craven Arms & Stokesay
            Via Woofferton
          THIRD CLASS
            2/8¼ Fare 2/8¼
Issued subject to the conditions&regulations set
out in theCompaniesTimeTables Bills&Notices
    CravenA.&S'say   CravenA.&S'say

947   947

21.   The train seen in picture 14 is ready to return to Woofferton at 4.46pm. Diesel and steam power was mixed for over 20 years. (Stephenson Locomotive Society)

22.   A through train from Kidderminster was recorded behind 2-6-2T no. 4175 in the mid-1950s. The Bath House at the Wells was open from 1862 to 1872, but from 1911 it was marketed in earnest. The locomotive was based mainly at Kidderminster from 1949 to 1964. (M.Whitehouse coll.)

23.   Looking in the same direction in September 1960, we see the passenger crossing and the milepost, showing five from Woofferton. (R.M.Casserley)

352   2nd-SINGLE SINGLE-2nd   352

Tenbury Wells to

Tenbury Wells   Tenbury Wells
Easton C. for L.H.   Easton C. for L.H.

EASTON COURT
(FOR LITTLE HEREFORD)

(W)   6d. Fare 6d.   (W)

For conditions see over For conditions see over-

24.   The Swan Hotel's horse drawn bus "met every train" until the early 1930s, when trips away became popular. The first coastal excursion was to Barry Island on 15th August 1926. On the right of this 1960 photograph is the 1913 provision for ladies. (H.C.Casserley)

25.   The arrangements for gentlemen are indicated here and in the next view. These are both from about 1961 and this one includes a train for cattle, a service that would soon be discontinued nationwide. (J.Moss/R.S.Carpenter coll.)

26.   Excursion destinations had once included the Kington Horse Show, the Birmingham Onion Fair and Ludlow Races. The 1878 signal box was in use until 28th April 1963. It had 20 levers from 1913. (J.Moss/R.S.Carpenter coll.)

```
          2nd-SINGLE  SINGLE-2nd
              Tenbury  Wells  to
  951   Tenbury Wells            Tenbury Wells   951
        EastonCt.forL.Hfd EastonCt.forL.H'f'd
        EASTON COURT   for Little Hereford
          (W)   8d    Fare    8d    (W)
        For conditions see over   For conditions see over
```

27.　　In pristine condition, no. W23W calls on 24th June 1961. The population had changed
little: 2080 in 1901 and 2015 in 1961. Gas lighting had been provided in 1905.
(G.Adams/M.J.Stretton coll.)

Great Western Railway
TENBURY TO
BEWDLEY
Via Tenbury and Bewdley.
FIRST CLASS
Issued subject to the conditions stated
on the Co's. Time Bills.　[8.]
Bewdley　　　　　Bewdley

344

28.   Bound for Woofferton is 0-6-0PT no. 3601, while 0-4-2T no. 1445 is propelling its coach to Kidderminster, not long before closure. The term "Wells" had been added on 4th November 1912. (M.J.Stretton coll.)

29.   Sectional warehouses (left) were provided in the 1950s for distribution of agricultural merchandise. Grass gradually crept over the tracks and goods traffic ceased on 6th January 1964. Lower right is another milepost; this shows 152¾, which was from Paddington. (Stations UK)

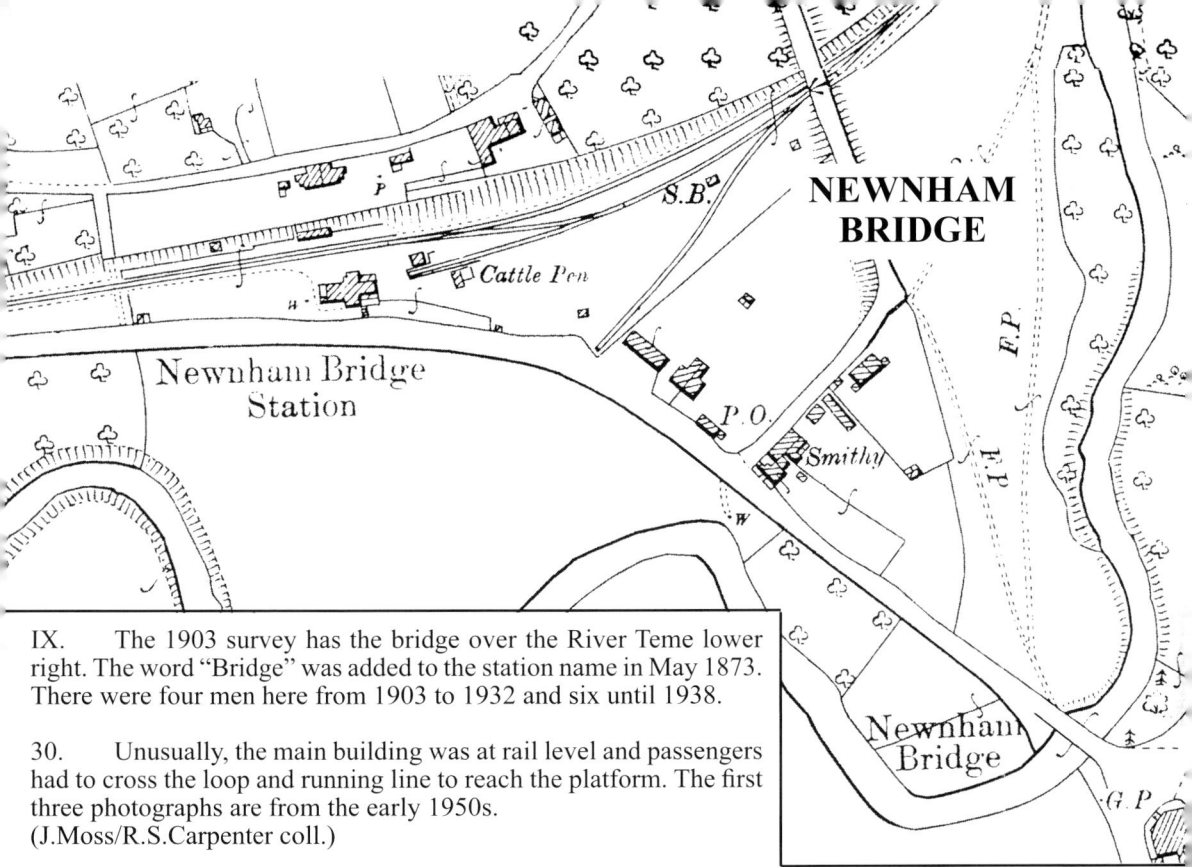

NEWNHAM BRIDGE

S.B.

Cattle Pen

Newnham Bridge
Station

P.O.

Smithy

F.P.

F.P.

Newnham
Bridge

G.P.

IX.   The 1903 survey has the bridge over the River Teme lower right. The word "Bridge" was added to the station name in May 1873. There were four men here from 1903 to 1932 and six until 1938.

30.   Unusually, the main building was at rail level and passengers had to cross the loop and running line to reach the platform. The first three photographs are from the early 1950s.
(J.Moss/R.S.Carpenter coll.)

31.   Here is the other end of one of the crossings and the waiting room with its lofty chimney. This station was extremely busy in the soft fruit season, with lorries often queuing down the road to unload. (J.Moss/R.S.Carpenter coll.)

Newham Bridge	1903	1913	1923	1933
Passenger tickets issued	12820	13398	12690	6577
Season tickets issued	*	*	9	6
Parcels forwarded	6528	8377	14239	6508
General goods forwarded (tons)	1084	1490	2758	4185
Coal and coke received (tons)	203	334	288	269
Other minerals received (tons)	2004	4678	2086	941
General goods received (tons)	1741	2350	1684	904
Trucks of livestock handled	127	45	33	40
(* not available)				

32.　　　Reference to the map shows two tracks under the bridge. This was rebuilt in 1930 to allow three, as the sidings had to be lengthened to cope with a great increase in traffic. The hut housed a 14-lever ground frame. (J.Moss/R.S.Carpenter coll.)

33.　　　The cattle pens are evident, but the 5-ton crane is out of view. This July 1961 picture reveals that there was a second crossing. The nearest was used by passengers and the other by road vehicles backing up to the platform. (R.G.Nelson/T.Walsh)

34.   We are now 149½ miles from London and a Woofferton-bound railcar stops for parcel traffic, probably soft fruit. (J.Peden/Stations UK)

35.   Our four final views are from 1961, the last full year of passenger operation. No. 3601 is working a Tenbury Wells to Kidderminster freight; this service continued until 1964. (J.Moss/R.S.Carpenter coll.)

36.   The panorama includes the weigh house (left) and another modern agricultural warehouse (right). The gates were well maintained to the end. (J.Moss/R.S.Carpenter coll.)

37. With scythes in hand, two men gather hay. It seems to have been stacked behind flat wagons, probably all condemned. The crane was of 5-ton capacity. The cottages once housed canal workers. (J.Moss/R.S.Carpenter coll.)

38. The goods loop was installed in 1914 and an intermediate electric token instrument allowed it to accommodate a goods train, while a passenger service passed. (R.G.Nelson/T.Walsh)

NEEN SOLLARS

X.   The 1904 survey shows no habitation nearby. The village recorded 206 residents in 1901. There was a staff of three from 1913 to 1932.

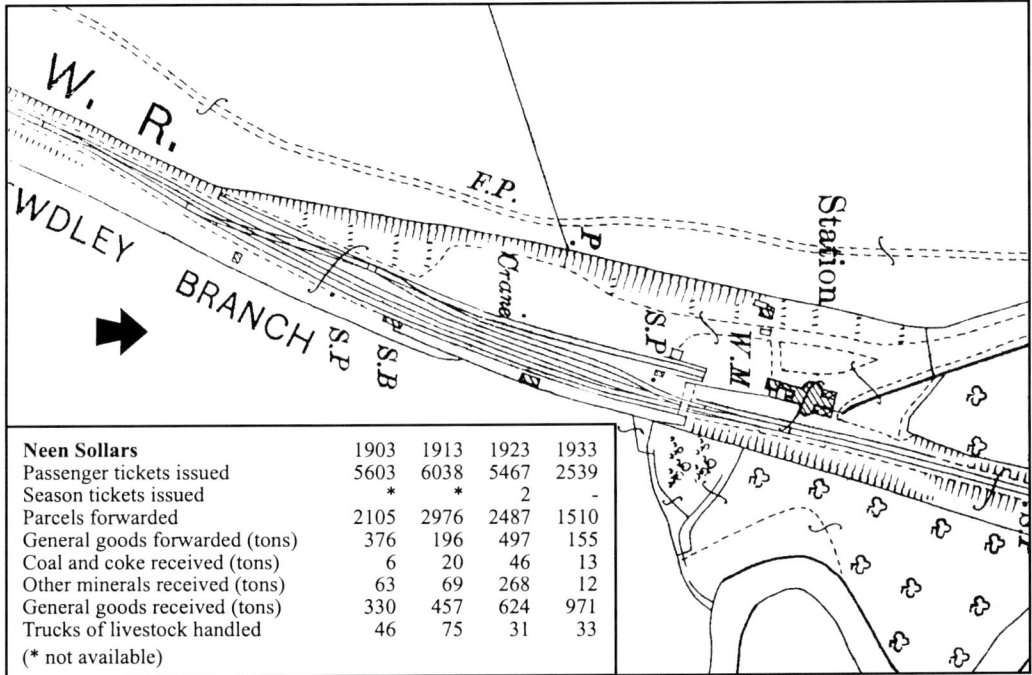

Neen Sollars	1903	1913	1923	1933
Passenger tickets issued	5603	6038	5467	2539
Season tickets issued	*	*	2	-
Parcels forwarded	2105	2976	2487	1510
General goods forwarded (tons)	376	196	497	155
Coal and coke received (tons)	6	20	46	13
Other minerals received (tons)	63	69	268	12
General goods received (tons)	330	457	624	971
Trucks of livestock handled	46	75	31	33
(* not available)				

39.   An early postcard shows the station to have staggered platforms linked by a board crossing. There had been only one platform until 1878. (Chambers coll./HMRS)

40.   A 1949 southward view from a railcar gives a rare glimpse of both platforms simultaneously. The 1878 platform (left) was taken out of use on 22nd August 1954, when the signal box closed. It had 16 levers until 1923, when a 23-lever frame was fitted. (J.Moss/R.S.Carpenter coll.)

41.   A Bewdley to Tenbury Wells train approaches sometime in August 1956 and a huddle of folk await it. The building was based on the reversal of the plan used at Newnham Bridge. The locomotive is probably no. 82008, the only BR class 3 2-6-2 tank allocated to Kidderminster at the time and never a prolific performer on this line. (Stephenson Locomotive Society)

42. No. W23W is bound for Tenbury Wells on 24th June 1961. Staffing ceased in the following month, but the cans of drinking water would still be required for the occupants of the house. (G.Adams/M.J.Stretton coll.)

43. The building remains in use as a dwelling, but is largely obscured in this northward view from July 1961. Goods service was maintained until 6th January 1964, although the yard was overgrown. (R.G.Nelson/T.Walsh)

CLEOBURY MORTIMER

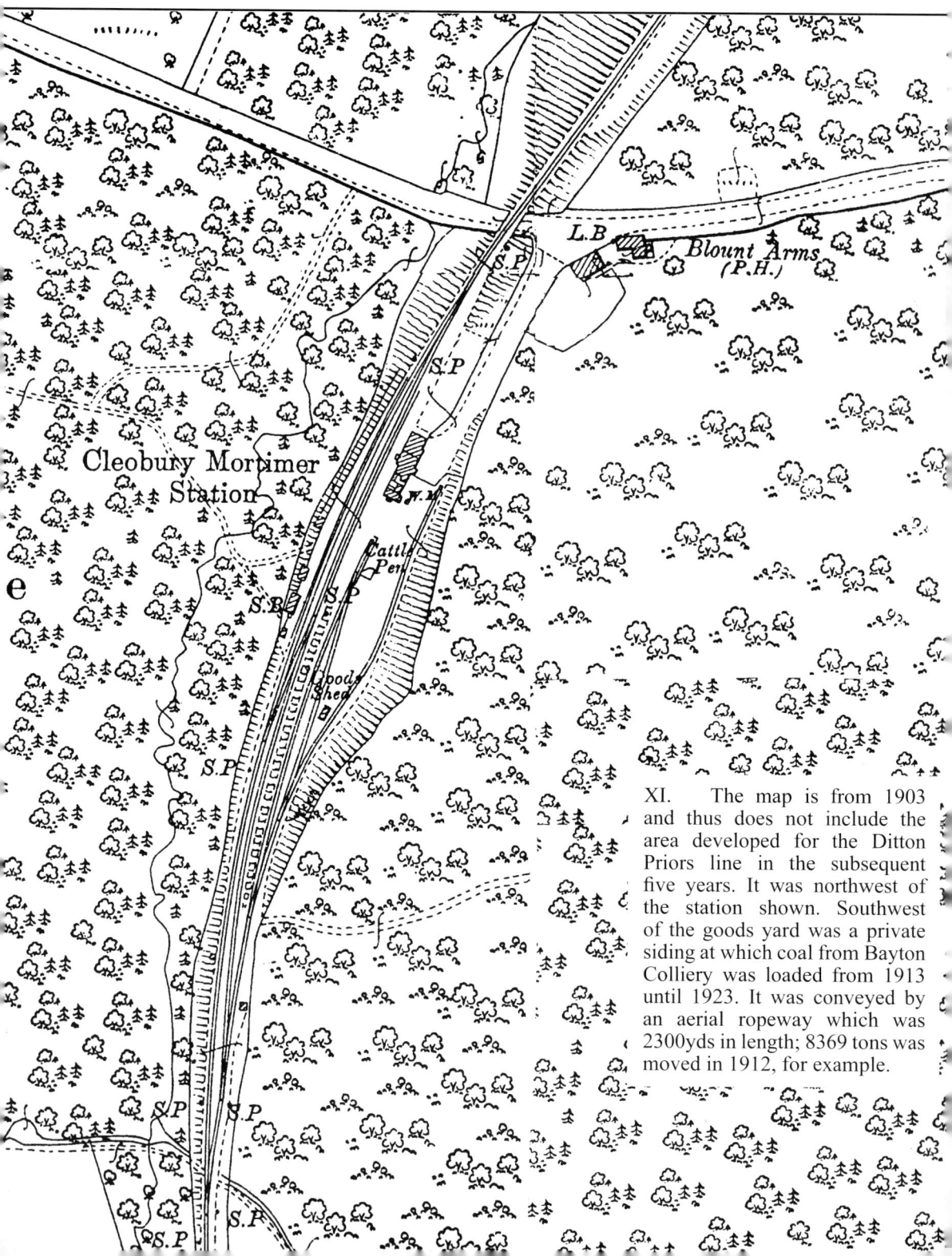

XI.   The map is from 1903 and thus does not include the area developed for the Ditton Priors line in the subsequent five years. It was northwest of the station shown. Southwest of the goods yard was a private siding at which coal from Bayton Colliery was loaded from 1913 until 1923. It was conveyed by an aerial ropeway which was 2300yds in length; 8369 tons was moved in 1912, for example.

44.   A northward view in August 1932 includes a train bound for Ditton Priors. There was a staff of eight here in 1913. (Mowat coll./Brunel University)

45.   No. 4586 is seen with the 4.40pm Kidderminster to Woofferton on 11th May 1938. Clerestory coaches would not be used for much longer. (R.S.Carpenter coll.)

46.	No. 6430 runs in from Kidderminster as the hollyhocks and shadows lengthen, on 10th September 1938. The lamp bracket shadow is particularly notable. The locomotive escaped the cutters torch for eventual residence on the Llangollen Railway.
(L.W.Perkins/F.A.Wycherley coll.)

Gt.Western Ry
CHEAP TICKET
For day of issue by
trains as advertised
Cleobury M'tmer to
LUDLOW
Via Tenbury Wells
THIRD CLASS
SEE BACK	W.D

47.   The signalman is seen from a Woofferton-bound railcar on 2nd July 1949. The 1908
signal box had a 65-lever frame and was in use until the end of goods traffic in 1965. The previous
box had 27 levers. The colliery siding was used by a brickworks from 1932.
(J.Moss/R.S.Carpenter coll.)

48. Taking water on 10th September 1949 is 2-6-2T no. 4586. It is working the 11.55am Woofferton to Kidderminster service. Unusually, one oil lamp is exposed. (H.C.Casserley)

(top right) 49. Seen on the same day is the recently nationalised 0-6-0 no. 2286, still awaiting its official smokebox number plate. In the goods yard is a coal wagon extended for the carriage of coke. This is probably the daily freight from Hereford to Stourbridge via Tenbury Wells. Motive power was provided by Hereford and Stourbridge depots on alternate days. (H.C.Casserley)

(right) 50. A panorama devoid of trains enables us to see from the Ditton Priors branch (left) across to the goods yard (right). Its single siding was level for safety reasons. (R.G.Nelson/T.Walsh)

51. A close-up in 1957 reveals that the shed was a former horse box. On the right is the grooms compartment; centre are two stable doors, but the lower parts fold down. (R.M.Casserley)

52. A 1955 photograph features a railcar bound for Kidderminster and a special at the long-disused Ditton Priors platform, hence the crowds. The town was almost two miles away.
(A.J.B.Dodd/P.Chancellor coll.)

(below) 53. A crisp view south features the irregular foot crossing, used by few in later years. The population dropped from 1810 in 1901 to 1304 in 1961.
(R.G.Nelson/T.Walsh)

54.   A fine panorama from the top of the cutting reveals well filled sidings on 18th March 1961 and the weighbridge at the far end of the nearest one. The building remains in use as a dwelling. (J.Langford)

Cleobury Mortimer	1903	1913	1923	1933
Passenger tickets issued	12958	15700	25853	12534
Season tickets issued	*	*	40	35
Parcels forwarded	8308	15001	17480	14051
General goods forwarded (tons)	2145	2233	3121	3045
Coal and coke received (tons)	313	3035	2526	1804
Other minerals received (tons)	1219	4482	2453	1579
General goods received (tons)	2839	3815	4144	2262
Trucks of livestock handled	114	274	154	80

(* not available)

55.   The curious paving of the main platform is emphasised in this southward view. Also clear is the parcel weighing machine but the canopy had been removed. (Stations UK)

56.   The prospective passengers' perspective presented familiar styling, but with an extra bedroom, as a late addition. The tank supplied the two "parachutes" seen in picture 53. A Ford Zodiac completes the period scene. (R.G.Nelson/T.Walsh)

Other views of this station can be found in pictures 76 to 83, these showing the branch side of the station.

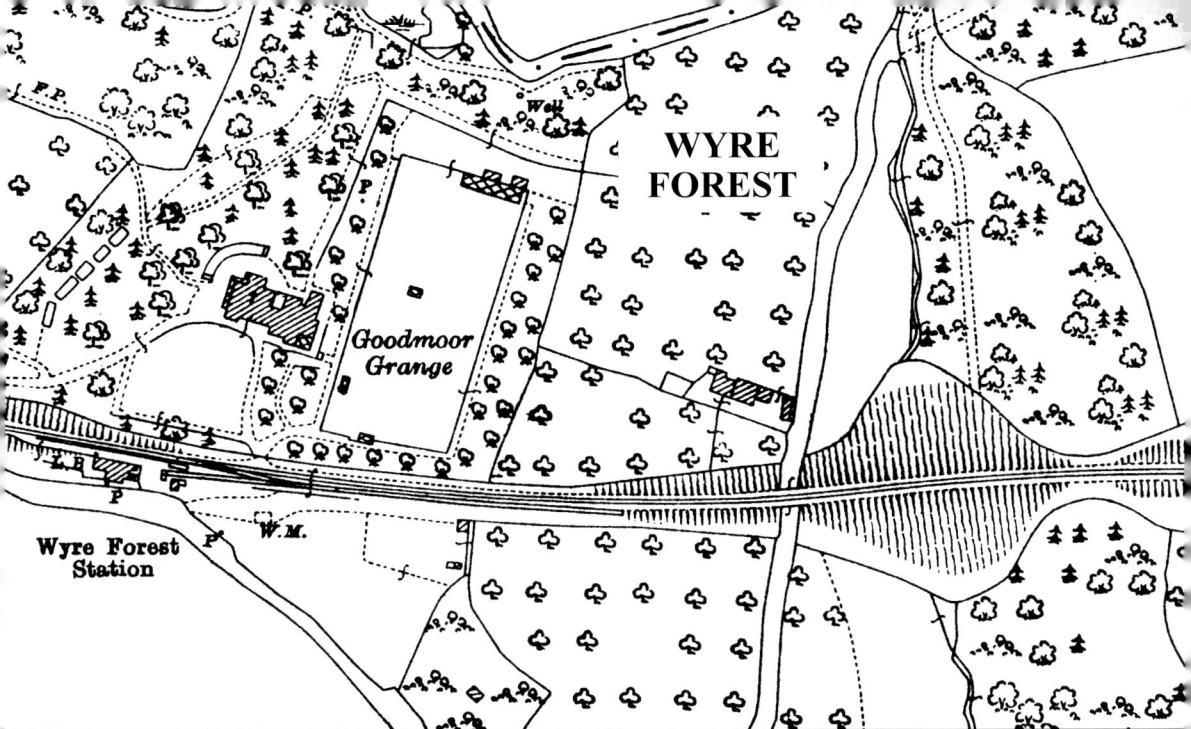

WYRE FOREST

Goodmoor Grange

Wyre Forest Station

XII.   The 1927 survey confirms the woodland setting of the station. A small stream runs under the massive embankment on the right. The county boundary is again close to the railway.

57.   The station did not open until 1st June 1869 and required the consent of the Office of Wood and Forest. This and the next photograph date from July 1957. (R.M.Casserley)

58.   Goods traffic did not begin until late in the 19th century, the main commodity being timber. However, in 1896 it was water pipes, to connect Welsh reservoirs to the Midlands. (R.M.Casserley)

Wyre Forest	1903	1913	1923	1933
Passenger tickets issued	5314	5948	5774	2751
Season tickets issued	*	*	16	-
Parcels forwarded	2617	2538	1386	1172
General goods forwarded (tons)		Goods Traffic included		37
Coal and coke received (tons)		with Cleobury Mortimer		131
Other minerals received (tons)		prior to 1926		101
General goods received (tons)	"	"	"	24
Trucks of livestock handled	"	"	"	-
(* not available)				

59.   One of the longest straight sections of track was west of the station and is seen in April 1959. The TELEPHONE sign offered the station 'phone to the public, the fee being paid to the staff after the call. (H.C.Casserley)

60.   The rural location is evident in this 1961 view. The staff of one was withdrawn on 31st July of that year. (J.Langford)

61.   The single siding was not used after staffing ceased, although goods trains passed through for another four years. (J.Moss/R.S.Carpenter coll.)

62.   The hut on the left housed the ground frame and most of the rodding from it is evident. Economy is obvious: the seats have no backs and the door for gentlemen has no screen. (J.Moss/ R.S.Carpenter coll.)

63.   Our final view is from 29th April 1961 and shows no. W22W working the 3.29pm from Bewdley. Peace and tranquility will soon return. (D.Johnson)

64.   This perfect profile is of a GWR 517 class 0-4-2T with a train of six-wheeled coaches on Dowles Bridge in about 1905. (Kidderminster Railway Museum)

65.   No. 3601 is passing over the River Severn in about 1959. The village of Dowles was never provided with a station or halt. The bridge spans were demolished in March 1966, but the piers are still standing. (A.W.V.Mace/Mile Post 92½)

66.   After leaving the east end of the bridge, trains curved south to run parallel to the Severn Valley line to Bewdley. This was initially higher than the other route and can be seen below the buffer of 2-6-2T no. 4153 on 29th May 1963. (Kidderminster Railway Museum)

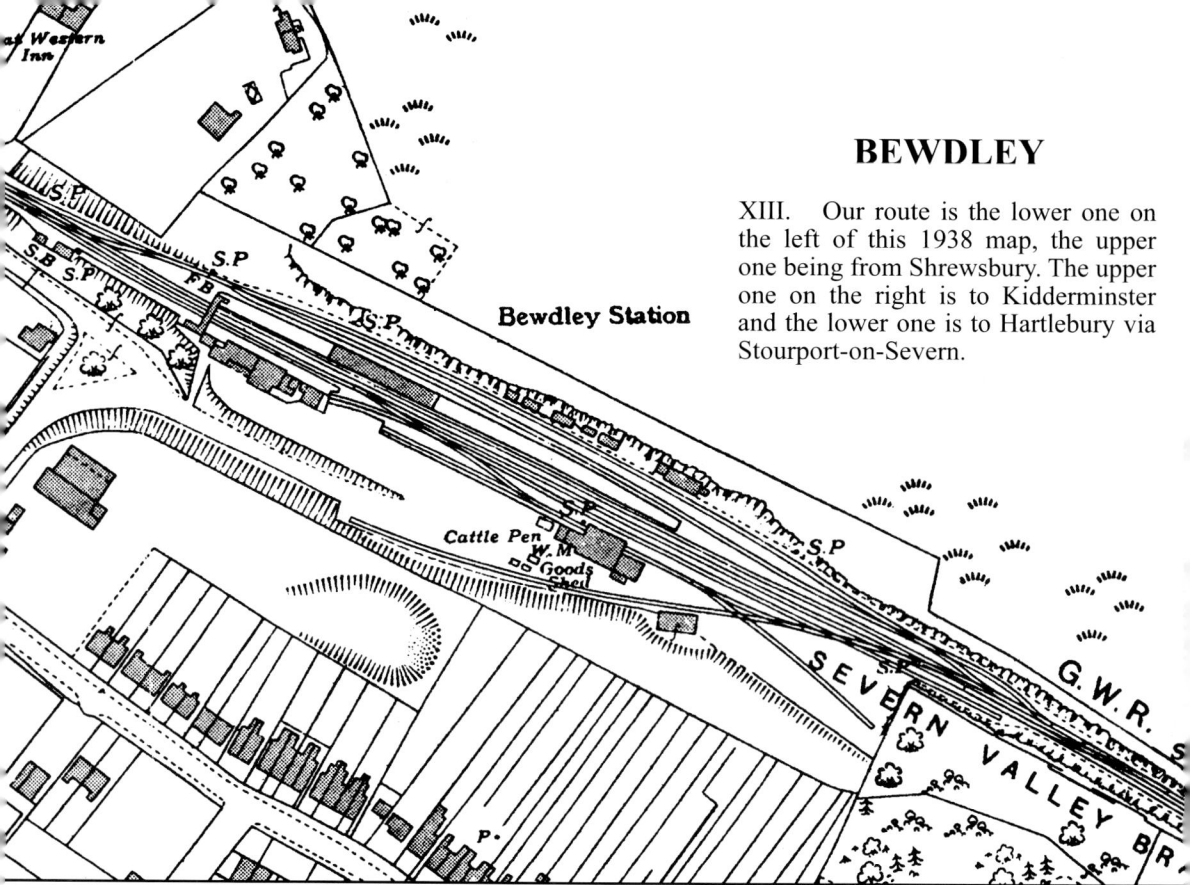

BEWDLEY

Bewdley Station

XIII.   Our route is the lower one on the left of this 1938 map, the upper one being from Shrewsbury. The upper one on the right is to Kidderminster and the lower one is to Hartlebury via Stourport-on-Severn.

67.   The original platform is on the left, the island one being built when the station became a junction in 1864. The 2-4-0T is probably bound for Hartlebury in about 1900, when most coaches were still lit by oil. (Kidderminster Railway Museum)

68.   Another early postcard and this is the view in the other direction, with a steam railmotor on the far side of the island platform. The covered footbridge was a welcome feature at many GWR junctions. (Lens of Sutton coll.)

69.   The two-tone valance had been repainted uniform cream when another postcard producer called. Note the sleepers were still tidily covered with ballast, a practice soon outlawed on safety grounds. (Kidderminster Railway Museum)

70.   At the north end of the station in the same era are two class 517 0-4-2Ts. The one on the left is probably bound for Shrewsbury while the other is likely to be destined for Tenbury Wells. The railmotor may be working Kidderminster-Bewdley-Hartlebury or the reverse, a common local service. (Kidderminster Railway Museum)

Other views of this station and the Severn Valley line can be seen in our *Kidderminster to Shrewsbury* album.

71.   At platform 1 (left) on 1st April 1961 is W22W having just arrived from Tenbury Wells. No. W23W will leave for Hartlebury at 10.35am. (J.Langford)

72.   The full length of platform 1 is evident and at the end of it is North box, which had 37 levers and was in use until May 1970. The two single lines northwards began near it. The goods yard closed on 1st February 1965 and passenger service was withdrawn on 5th January 1970. (Lens of Sutton coll.)

73.   The station was reopened by the Severn Valley Railway on 18th May 1974 and all its facilities were admirably restored to exceptional standards. Waiting to return to Bridgnorth on 12th September is 0-6-0PT no. 5764. (T.Heavyside)

A 00285
S.OO

SPECIAL 2nd
CHEAP DAY

Kidderminster
Via BEWDLEY CURVE
TO
Neen Sollars
FARE 1/6 (W)
Kidderminster
For Condition See Over

B5—Williamson, Printer, Ashton

74.   The renovated booking hall is a classic example of the best in heritage railway restorations, as is no. 4930 *Hagley Hall*, which was working the 11.00 to Bridgnorth on 2nd May 1982. (D.H.Mitchell)

75.   The steam era has been faithfully recreated in every aspect of railway operation, including replica freight trains. Seen on 18th April 1993, ex-LMS class 3F 0-6-0T is about to pass North box, itself faithfully restored. (T.Heavyside)

2. Ditton Priors Branch

CLEOBURY MORTIMER

───────→ 76. The CMDPLR bought two 0-6-0STs from Manning Wardle in 1908 and named them *Cleobury* and *Burwarton*. The GWR rebuilt them as seen, removed the names and numbered them 28 and 29 respectively. This is the latter in about 1933. (R.S.Carpenter coll.)

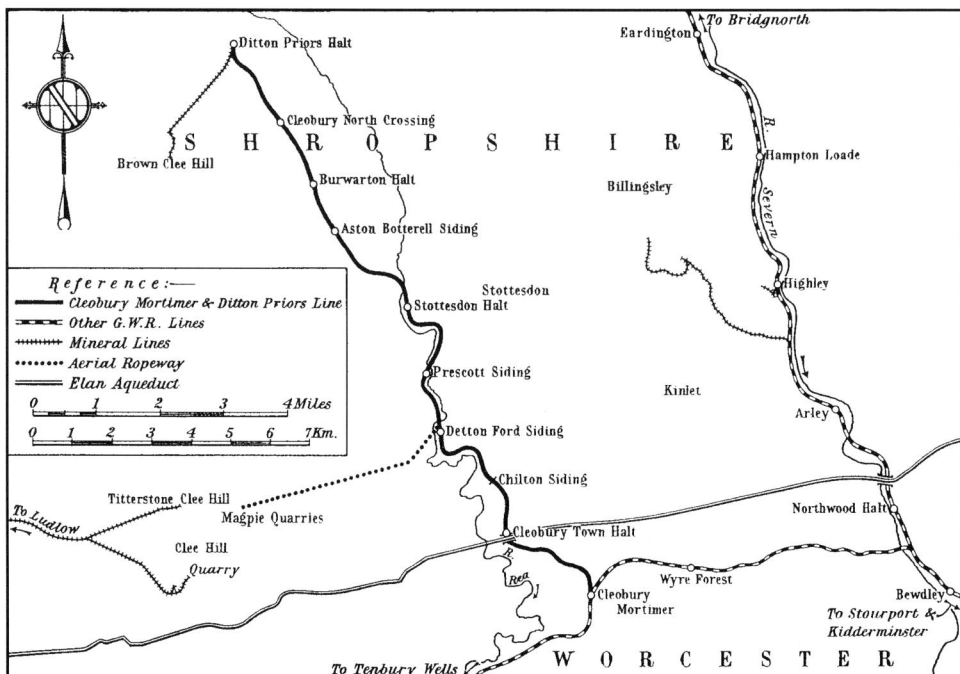

XIV.   Branch station names are as at their closure in 1938. (Railway Magazine)

───────→ 77.   No. 28 stands at the branch platform on 11th May 1938 with the GWR sign still suggesting that the branch was not theirs. The line's original four ex-North London Railway coaches were replaced by elderly GWR ones in 1926. (R.S.Carpenter coll.)

CLEOBURY MORTIMER
CHANGE FOR
DITTON PRIORS RAILWAY

78.   The initial curve of the branch passed over a road bridge and it is seen on the same day. There were also connections to the branch loop, south of the signal box, from the Tenbury Wells line. (R.S.Carpenter coll.)

79.   The bridge of 1864 was of steel construction and is seen through the brick arch of the branch railway in 1938. The town was more than one mile to the west. The road was numbered A4117 in 1919. The brick bridge arch was blown up in 1969. (L.W.Perkins/F.A.Wycherley coll.)

GWR SPECIAL NOTICE

DISCONTINUANCE OF
PASSENGER TRAIN SERVICE

BETWEEN

CLEOBURY MORTIMER

AND

DITTON PRIORS

The Great Western Railway give notice that on and from MONDAY, SEPTEMBER 26th, 1938, the Passenger Train service on the above Line will be withdrawn and the following trains cancelled :—

9.30 a.m. Cleobury Mortimer to Ditton Priors.
2.24 p.m. (Wednesdays only) Cleobury Mortimer to Ditton Priors.
5.20 p.m. Cleobury Mortimer to Ditton Priors.
11.10 a.m. Ditton Priors to Cleobury Mortimer.
3.50 p.m. (Wednesdays only) Ditton Priors to Cleobury Mortimer.
6.23 p.m. Ditton Priors to Cleobury Mortimer.

The Platforms at the undermentioned places will be closed to Passengers —

CLEOBURY TOWN HALT   ASTON BOTTERELL SIDING
DETTON FORD SIDING   BURWARTON HALT
PRESCOTT SIDING   CLEOBURY NORTH CROSSING
STOTTESDON HALT   DITTON PRIORS HALT

The Company will continue to run one Goods train in each direction over the Line on week-days only, and so afford facilities for the conveyance of Parcels traffic, Minerals, Livestock and General Merchandise to and from the above-mentioned places.

Particulars of the arrangements may be obtained on application to the Station Master, Cleobury Mortimer, Mr. J. E. POTTER, Divisional Superintendent, Worcester (Shrub Hill Station) (Telephone 1530), or Mr. J. A. WARREN-KING, District Goods Manager, Worcester (Shrub Hill Station) (Telephone 1530).

PADDINGTON STATION,
July, 1938.

JAMES MILNE,
General Manager.

XV. Closure notice.

80.   A train bound for Tenbury Wells is on the left on 10th September 1938, worked by 0-6-0PT no. 6430. The branch train will leave for Ditton Priors at 5.20pm. (Stephenson Locomotive Society)

(below) 81. The branch train is seen behind no. 28 on 24th September 1938, the photographer being on the signal bracket seen in picture 78. This was the last day of public service. Note that the canopy seen in the first group of pictures is not present, it was probably a wartime addition. The 5.20pm 4-coach train stands at the short platform, with 0-6-0PT no. 29 and a party of mourners. Two coaches were normally more than adequate. (A.N.H.Glover/F.A.Wycherley coll.)

82.   The Stephenson Locomotive Society ran a special train on the branch on 21st May 1955 and it was hauled by 0-6-0 no. 2516. Also visible is the 5-ton goods crane. (T.J.Edgington)

83.   Due to the wartime emergency, two camping coaches were berthed here for Royal Navy staff in 1941-42. The branch platform and loop are seen on 6th July 1961.
(R.G.Nelson/T.Walsh)

CLEOBURY TOWN HALT

84.   The contractors yard and engine shed are seen before the line opened and the headquarters building of the railway is in the background. (A.Dudman coll.)

85.   The status of "halt" was bestowed in 1926, the stop being little used as the town was more than ½ mile distant. The 0-6-0ST *Cleobury* is at the same location, running north, with the NLR coaches. Both locomotives were rebuilt as 0-6-0PTs by the GWR in 1923-24.
(A.Dudman coll.)

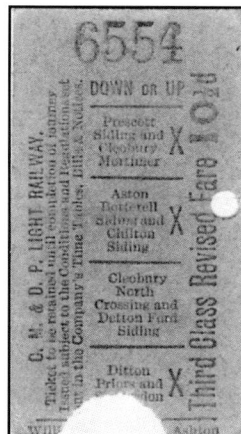

86.   The engine shed is in the distance in this northward view from 30th March 1938. Two wagons belong to D&F Fellows, coal and coke factors of Cradley Heath, one is from Littleton Collieries and the other was based here. (R.S.Carpenter coll.)

87.   Arriving on the same day is no. 29 with the 2.24pm, Wednesdays only, from Cleobury Mortimer to Ditton Priors. Curiously neither building was on the platform. (R.S.Carpenter coll.)

88.   It is September 1938 and no. 29 waits by the smoke blackened oil lamp intended to illuminate the coal stage. Further coal is stored in the wagons, beyond the 1917 shed, which had closed in July 1938. (L.W.Perkins/F.A.Wycherley coll.)

A 00079

S.00
FARE

1/7N

GREAT WESTERN RAILWAY
RAILMOTOR CAR.

Issued subject to the Conditions and
Regulations set out in the Company's Time
Tables, Bills and Notices.
NOT TRANSFERABLE.

Cleobury
Mortimer

Cleobury
Town Halt

Chilton Siding

Detton Ford
Siding

Prescott
Siding

Stottesdon
Halt

Aston
Botterell Sid'g

burwarton
Halt

Cleobury,
NorthCrossing

Ditton
Priors Halt

Cleobury Mortimer

0033

DOWN or UP

O. M. & D. P. Light Railway

Third Class

CHILD'S

TICKET

Revised Fare

8½ 10d

Ticket to be retained until completion of journey.
Issued subject to the Conditions and Regulations set
out in the Company's Time Tables, Bills & Notices.

Williamson, Printer, Ashton

89.   This panorama from the same month reveals the simple layout of the goods loop, with extensions at each end, and one siding to the loco shed. The weigh office is by Burwarton's sign and their office was opposite. They also dealt in building materials.
(Stephenson Locomotive Society)

90.   The final passenger train to Ditton Priors was the 5.29 on 24th September 1938. It was also probably the last trip for the coaches. (R.S.Carpenter coll.)

91.   A 1947 photograph includes Naval stores, a crane and a Bedford lorry. By this time, engines were provided from Kidderminster shed. The station was built from concrete panels produced at the Abdon Quarry Company's works, near Ditton Priors station. The shed in picture 88 was built likewise, as was one for LSWR locos at Salisbury. (Stations UK)

92.   The special train on 21st May 1955 called briefly and the level crossing gates were photographed. In the foreground is a hand-cranked grindstone for sharpening scythes and other tools. (Stations UK)

93.   By the time of this photograph from July 1961, the gates had rotted or been involved in a collision. Two Admiralty diesel locomotives had worked the branch since 31st September 1957. (R.G.Nelson/T.Walsh)

CHILTON SIDING

94.   This view north is from March 1938 and features a small platform, which was not listed in public timetables. This stop was also known as Nene Savage and was for the benefit of a local resident. (R.S.Carpenter coll.)

DETTONFORD SIDING

95   Two photographs from 1938 show the facilities on offer. For passengers there was one oil lamp and for freight there was one goods loop and a siding from it at its north end. (R.S.Carpenter coll.)

96.   The siding served this aerial ropeway from Magpie Quarries from 1908. It conveyed dhustone for road making. It had seven miles of rope on 56 trestles and was reported as closed in 1928. (R.S.Carpenter coll.)

PRESCOTT HALT

97.   The sign did not declare this to be a halt, but some timetables listed it as Prescott Siding. It trailed on the west side for northbound trains; the platform was on the east side, north of the siding. (R.S.Carpenter coll.)

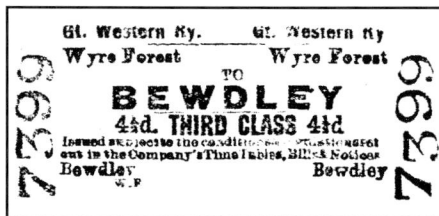

Gt. Western Ry.	Gt. Western Ry
Wyre Forest	Wyre Forest
	TO
BEWDLEY	
4½d. THIRD CLASS 4½d	
Issued subject to the conditions and regulations set	
out in the Company's Time Tables, Bills & Notices	
Bewdley	Bewdley

STOTTESDON HALT

98.   Another 1938 view and this includes a crossing for carts and lorries to load or unload. It was designated a station for many years. Flat bottom rail prevails. (R.S.Carpenter coll.)

99.   Looking north in 1961, we see the full length of the loop, plus the remains of the cattle dock at the near end of it. Bullhead rail is now evident. (R.G.Nelson/T.Walsh)

ASTON BOTTERELL HALT

100.   The siding runs to the south and is seen in 1938 with the usual lamp and locked hut. This was another platform created to serve the small local community. (R.S.Carpenter coll.)

BURWARTON

101.   A rare sign of activity on the branch in 1938 involves the track gang. Their jack and the platform scales are evident. The sleepers have seen better days. (R.S.Carpenter coll.)

102.   No. 29 was recorded northbound on 10th September 1938. As elsewhere, the goods loop had short sidings at each end. On the left is the lamp room. (L.W.Perkins/F.A.Wycherley coll.)

Gt. Western Ry.   Gt. Western Ry.
CLEOBURY   CLEOBURY
MORTIMER   MORTIMER
TO
BEWDLEY
6d, PARLY. (3rdCls.) 6d.
Issued subject to the conditions & regulations set out in the Company's Time Tables Books and Bills.   (C. G.)
Bewdley   Bewdley

4074

103.   A 1955 record shows no signs of recent local use. We have now climbed into thinly populated agricultural countryside, approaching 600ft above sea level. (T.J.Edgington)

104.   Seen in 1963, the ownership is clear, but few knew that there were only two years left for the line. The track seems in good order here. (B.W.L.Brooksbank)

ADMIRALTY · PROPERTY
NO
ADMITTANCE

CLEOBURY NORTH CROSSING

105.   This was the only station on the branch devoid of a siding. The village was almost ten miles from Cleobury Mortimer, but only a little to the west of the station. Seen in about 1930, the gates were the responsibility of the fireman. (Mowat coll./Brunel University)

106.   This was a request stop in later years and is seen in 1938. The second sign board carries an advertisement for the *Daily Mirror* and the other essential for life is in the foreground, the water carrier. (R.S.Carpenter coll.)

107.   Here was another building produced from locally manufactured concrete components. The gates carried red-painted oil lamps with red lenses, but had no warning discs, probably because of the low speed limit. The water in the cans contained trout from the nearby hatcheries. (R.S.Carpenter coll.)

108.   No. 29 had been the first engine to be fitted with a spark arrester for safety when hauling ammunition trains. This took place a few days after war was declared. Also soon thereafter, this stand pipe was erected at the approach to the exchange sidings for the RNAD, where Admiralty diesels took over the trains. This is the SLS special on 21st May 1955. (T.J.Edgington)

109.   At almost the same location, near Kennel Crossing, we witness Admiralty no. 35 with assorted stock for the RNAD in 1965. Its end was nigh. (A.Muckley)

DITTON PRIORS HALT

110.   The terminus is seen prior to the GWR takeover, with two of the former NLR coaches and one of the company's two brake vans. Few termini were termed a halt; this applied from 1923. (Lens of Sutton coll.)

2nd-SINGLE SINGLE-2nd
Tenbury Wells to
Tenbury Wells   Tenbury Wells
NeenSollars   Neen Sollars
NEEN SOLLARS
(W)   Fare 1/6   (W)
For conditions see over For conditions see over
1648   1648
1/6

111.   The history of this van is not recorded, but no. 1 lasted into GWR days, just. It was soon scrapped. The company owned 22 open wagons, but the GWR scrapped most of them. (Lens of Sutton coll.)

112.   *Cleobury* was Manning Wardle's no. 1735 and was a successful performer on the steeply graded branch. The GWR alterations included a reduced footplate and this necessitated provision of specially shortened shovels. It is seen with the 9.15am from Cleobury Mortimer on 1st May 1920. (K.Nunn/LCGB coll.)

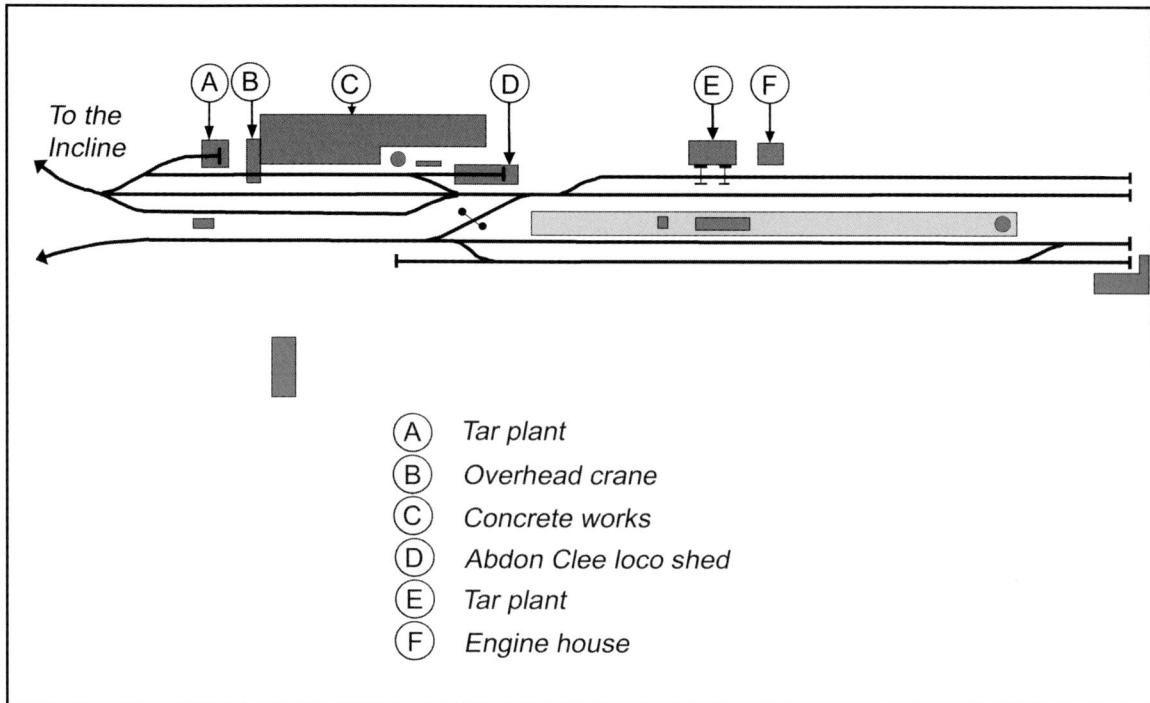

A — Tar plant
B — Overhead crane
C — Concrete works
D — Abdon Clee loco shed
E — Tar plant
F — Engine house

XVI. Track diagram until 1936.

XVII. Abdon Quarry track diagram.

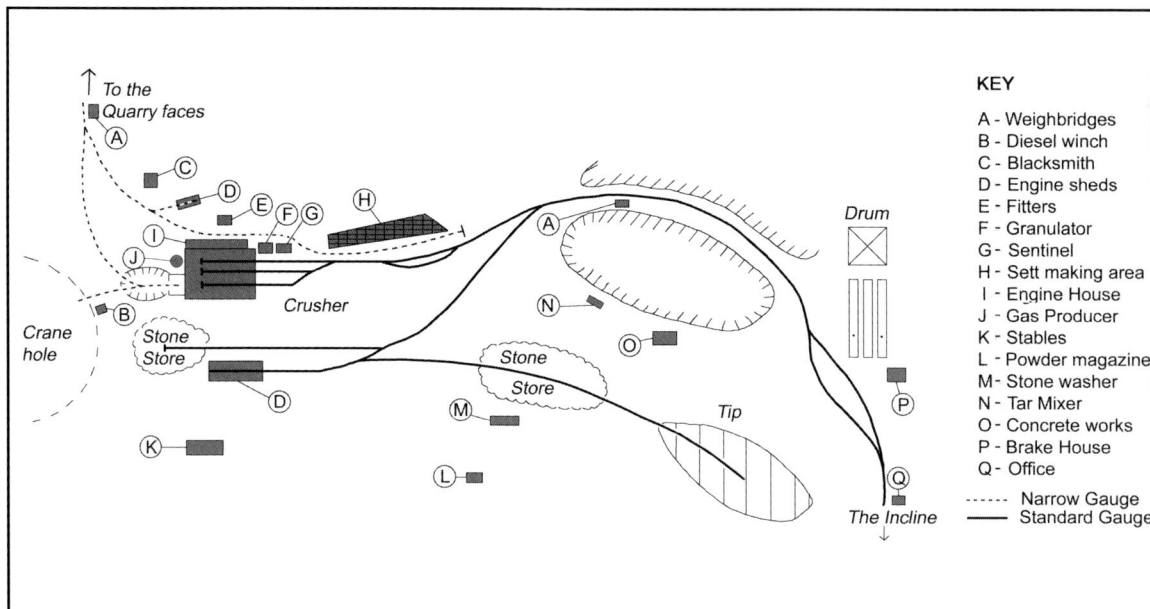

KEY

A - Weighbridges
B - Diesel winch
C - Blacksmith
D - Engine sheds
E - Fitters
F - Granulator
G - Sentinel
H - Sett making area
I - Engine House
J - Gas Producer
K - Stables
L - Powder magazine
M - Stone washer
N - Tar Mixer
O - Concrete works
P - Brake House
Q - Office

----- Narrow Gauge
——— Standard Gauge

113.   The incline from the station up to Abdon Quarry is seen in August 1932. It was self
acting, with a braked drum at the top. Horse traction was used initially, railway ballast, road stone
and setts being the main products. Hudswell Clark 0-6-0ST no. 313 *Fleetwood* was the usual
locomotive at the top. There was also a 2ft gauge system in the quarry.
(Mowat coll./Brunel University)

114.   Manning Wardle 0-6-0ST no. 729 *Kingswood* was usually to be found shunting the lower
level, at Ditton Priors. A passenger train is in the background, sometime before the quarry closed
in June 1936. It had a third loco called *Trent* at one period, but little is known about it.
(Lens of Sutton coll.)

115.　The view of the end of the branch is from about 1935, when old GWR coaches were in use. The loop could not be used for unloading goods, as it was required for running round. (Stations UK)

116.   A mixed train including two wagons has arrived behind no. 28. On the right, wagons stand on the Abdon Quarry's own tracks. (Lens of Sutton coll.)

117.   No. 29 is assembling a down train so that the coaches are at the front. These had steam heating, unlike the NLR ones. The date is 30th March 1938. (R.S.Carpenter coll.)

118.   No. 29 waits to depart on 10th September 1938 and peace will return to this little visited outpost of the mighty GWR. Its accountants had woken up to the losses by that time. (L.W.Perkins/F.A.Wycherley coll.)

2nd · SINGLE   SINGLE · 2nd

Woofferton to

Woofferton   Woofferton

Easton C. for L.H.   Easton C. for L.H

EASTON COURT for Little Hereford

(W)   6d   Fare   6d   (W)

For conditions see over   For conditions see over

1944   1944

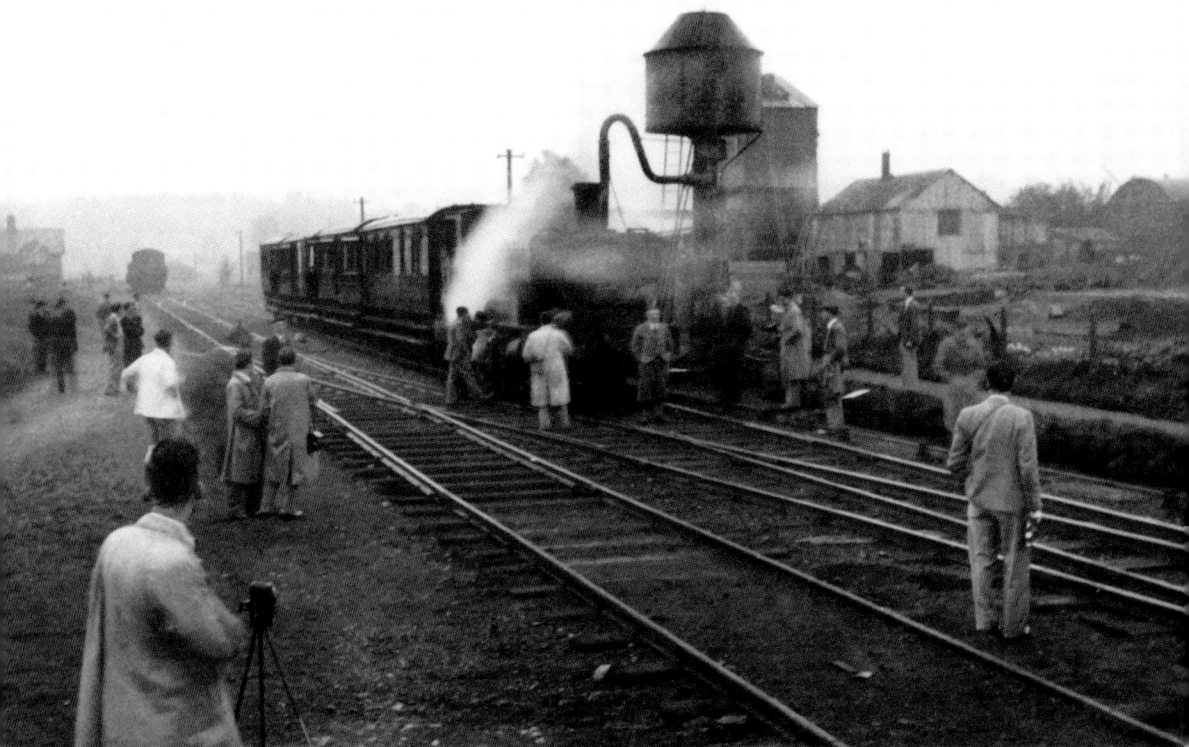

119.   The last day of passenger operation was marred by drizzle. The train will leave at 6.50pm behind no. 29. On the right is part of the quarry's engine shed and the tarmac production plant. (R.S.Carpenter coll.)

120.   The Admiralty's diesel no. 35 was of Ruston & Hornsby manufacture and was of class 165DS. The photograph is from 1965, by which time the branch was well past its unexpected peak of prosperity. (A.Muckley)

MP Middleton Press

EVOLVING THE ULTIMATE RAIL ENCYCLOPEDIA

Easebourne Lane, Midhurst, West Sussex.
GU29 9AZ   Tel:01730 813169

www.middletonpress.co.uk   email:info@middletonpress.co.uk
A-978 0 906520   B- 978 1 873793   C- 978 1 901706   D-978 1 904474   E- 978 1 906008

OOP Out of print at time of printing - Please check availability   BROCHURE AVAILABLE SHOWING NEW TITLES